SIMPLY ASTROLOGY

Rosângela Alvarenga
Translation Rafa Lombardino

SIMPLY ASTROLOGY

1st Edition
POD

Petrópolis
KBR
2013

Translation **Rafa Lombardino**
Text Edition **Noga Sklar**
Cover **Google Archive**

ISBN: 978-85-8180-200-8

KBR Editora Digital Ltda.
www.kbrdigital.com.br
www.facebook.com/kbrdigital
atendimento@kbrdigital.com.br
24 2222.3491

OCC002000 - Astrology

Rosangela Alvarenga is a Brazilian psychoanalyst and astrologer. She graduated from Medical School at Federal University of Rio de Janeiro (UFRJ) in 1981. She went to the Freudian School of Rio de Janeiro and worked under the supervision of Dr. Eduardo Mascarenhas for four years. Between 1984 and 2010, she wrote the Astrology column for the Brazilian newspaper *O Globo,* the most important in the country. She works as a psychologist and astrologer in her private practice in Rio, teaches Astrology classes, and publishes horoscopes on her website at http://www.astrologiaecia.com.br.

Email: ro.alvarenga@globo.com
Twitter: @HoroscopodaRosa

AUTHOR'S NOTE

This book is intended for people who wish to be introduced to the science/art known as Astrology. I can imagine your motives: pure and simple curiosity; justifying to yourself why you read the horoscope in magazines and newspapers, looking for some signs destiny has in store for you on that particular day; understanding the mysterious language of the stars and planets; a friend told you he got an astral chart done and learned incredible things about himself or his life; you want to know if your current or potential partner's sign is a match to yours, or you have been studying the occult and are interested in self-knowledge and self-development.

Of course I have not covered all the possibilities, and hope you understand if your case isn't any of the above. Whatever your reason may be, I'll try to share a little bit of my experience in Astrology with you.

TABLE OF CONTENTS

Astrological Symbols
Used In This Book

ARIES	TAURUS	GEMINI	CANCER	LEO
♈	♉	♊	♋	♌

VIRGO	LIBRA	SCORPIO	SAGITTARIUS
♍	♎	♏	♐

CAPRICORN	AQUARIUS	PISCES
♑	♒	♓

SUN	MOON	MERCURY	VENUS	MARS
☉	☽	☿	♀	♂

JUPITER	SATURN	URANUS
♃	♄	♅

NEPTUNE	PLUTO
♆	♇

Part I
Preliminaries

CHAPTER 1 - WHERE DOES ASTROLOGY COME FROM?

There was a time in history when humans really became *human*. In other words, they magically became aware of themselves and the world around them. "We are unclothed," Adam exclaimed in Paradise, expressing his perplexity. Nothing would be the same again. Adam even repented and covered his genitals with a fig leaf... It was a warning flag! Anyway, we know how the story ends: He saw, and was seen. There was no turning back. He needed to understand. Now. And it wasn't that simple.

There were no words to relieve the suffering of the primitive man. Today, it is easy to look up at the sky and say, "Sky." However, can you imagine how crazy it must have been to look at the world around you and not being able to name anything?! It is the same as contemplating chaos!

There was only Me (naked) and a bunch of non-Mes. Frightening! The first night of awareness, as perceived by the newborn Me, must have been of endless darkness... Hell—if only Hell could have been imagined back then. This newborn Me remained alert, shaking, and suddenly, amid darkness, there were pale promises of light somewhere, there... A new day: plenty of light to reveal all shapes and colors.

Without any recollections, the newborn Me thought he was in what could be called Paradise. But, then, again, the light went away. No! Don't go away! It'll get dark... It is dark. Now the newborn Me had memories and remembered darkness. And so he kept observing darkness, light, darkness, light.

The time went by. Eras went by, perhaps. And the newborn Me reached a conclusion—albeit a wordless one: after darkness, there is light. Then, darkness comes again, and so on and so forth. You can imagine how humans had to go a long way trying to understand the world they lived in. And we keep trying, to this day.

Recent studies suggest that primitive men looked at the sky for an explanation for the natural phenomena they constantly had to deal with: day, night, thunder, storm, wind, heat, cold, drought, and flood. They probably tried to find something that repeated itself to become a reference, to show some order amid the apparent chaos. Bone scripts from the Ice Age have been found to support this point of view, and suggest that men were already aware of lunar cycles (moon phases) 32,000 years ago. There are also Egyptian star cards that date back to 4,200 b.C.

More recently, fragments of a document that survived the kingdom of the Sargon of Akkad (2,334-2,279 b.C.) show that predictions were made according to the position of the sun, moon, five known planets, and a series of phenomena, including comets and meteorites.

Astrology is believed to have originated in Sumer around 3,000 b.C. The word "Astrology" comes from the Greek: *aster* means "stars" and *logos* means "account, report, reason, definition, rational faculty, and proportion."

Astrology was originally conceived by the Sumerian,

probably in the city of Ur, which is supposedly the birthplace of Abraham and was founded in the fourth millennium b.C. in north Mesopotamia.

The Sumerian were greatly interested in observing the sky and saw it as a large black dome made of silk to which stars were attached, as if they were shiny adornments. However, they noticed that, in addition to the Sun and the Moon, there were five stars that seemed to move faster than others: They were planets, more precisely, Mercury, Venus, Mars, Jupiter, and Saturn. These were the seven celestial bodies that received special attention. The Sumerian analyzed their position in the sky and believed their arrangement to be the work of Gods, for the benefit of Mankind.

Later, the Chaldeans developed Astrology as it is known today, and, for centuries, it remained the same without much change to its basic premises. Stars were grouped in constellations to serve as markers for the movement of planets. The Zodiac, also known as the Way of Anu, was the route followed by the Sun, Moon, and planets, always with the same mass of stars—or zodiac constellations. Dividing the Zodiac in twelve parts may have been a result of the Chaldeans dividing the day in twelve parts, each of them lasting two hours.

By mid-7th century b.C., Astrology started to spread throughout Greece. *Babyloniaca*, a book written in Greek by Chaldean astrologist Berossus, approximately in 280 b.C., was the main title responsible for spreading the word.

From the Middle Ages to the Modern Era, what we now call "Scientific Revolution" took place. During said period, men realized they had built their own universe, and the medieval view of a world controlled by Gods was discredited. Later on, the paths followed by Astrology and Astronomy were inevitably split when the Sun—not the Earth—was found to be the center of the universe around which celestial bodies rotated.

With the increased interest in scientific investigation methods, which are inductive and deductive, Astrology experienced a decline in its prestige, since its premises were not verifiable by scientific methods—results cannot be reproduced in a laboratory setting.

For years, Astrology was under the stigma of "non-scientific" knowledge, whose roots were in men's mystic and superstitious past. While the official science was unveiling more and more mysteries from the physical universe, Astrology insisted in interpreting celestial events more or less the same way as it had in the remote past. Interpretations from astrologers weren't even shaken by the discovery that the Sun—not the Earth—was the center of the universe.

Despite its roots in ancient times, astrological premises *still* cannot be proved scientifically. The paradox is that only recently, at the end of the 20th century, some scientists have turned their attention to the fascinating standards of rhythmic and cyclic behavior of men, animals, and nature itself. And it is exactly in this cyclic feature of our existence that astrological knowledge has been based on from the very beginning.

Chapter 2 - Astrology and Life Cycles

In addition to the first cycles that Astrology was aware of—day and night, seasons of the year, moon phases—we now know about the cycles of the brain, hormones, cardiac activity, sleep and vigil. Patterns of fatigue and recovery, stress and relaxation have been identified in hormonal and gland activities. At another level, sociologists, economists, anthropologists, and environmentalists have detected additional cycles in large groups and societies whose periodicity may vary from seconds to decades.

All of these cycles may be regulated by hidden "clocks," and their interaction with one another can be observed as well. There are organizations dedicated to studying cycles and setting statistic patterns of different natures. Their studies sometimes achieve surprising results, so much so that the president of one of these foundations has stated that Mankind seems to be subject to an enormous force—maybe a cosmic one—that determines our actions. These forces seem to define periods of prosperity and depression, highs and lows seen not only in agriculture, but also in mining and industrial activities, thus controlling even interest rates and the stock market!

It is clear each day that things are somehow connected or related and that we can only obtain partial results when we study an isolated phenomenon under unnatural conditions. The most current trend in human thought is to consider the Universe as a whole and its parts as constantly interacting with one another. In other words, one isolated event has implications on all other parts to a larger or smaller degree.

Therefore, it isn't a stretch to think that certain celestial events may resonate with issues from our own little worlds... But we can talk about this later. For now, modern astrologers are still based on old "folklore" and analogical methods that have been enhanced by a deep study of the intertwined nature of each and every cycle.

Even without the vast knowledge available to our contemporary culture, the first astrologers reached surprising conclusions by following a path of simplicity. By observing the sky, they soon realized the most evident cyclic patterns. They noticed that something that begins is always... beginning. If it has matured and reached its apex, it's because it has already begun. If it is in decline, it's because it has already begun and reached its apex.

Now, let's think about it together: The beginning of everything depends on a very high potential of concentrated energy, enough to trigger it and conquer inertia—the tendency to remain the same. And everything that peaks tends to reach stability for a moment, before it finally starts to decline.

The intertwined nature of cycles is expressed with poetry and precision in the *I Ching*, the book that summarizes most of the Chinese ancient wisdom. It is not because men were in their primitive stages of development that they lacked intelligence or sagacity.

The first astrologers took as a reference the apparent

cycle of the Sun around the Earth—apparent, but no measurable back then. The starting point was the famous Equinox Point, which is the beginning of spring in the northern hemisphere, and fall in the southern hemisphere. The cycle was initially divided into four parts: beginning, apex, decline, and fall. Later, each part was divided into three stages, each representing a transition from one phase to another. Consequently, the Zodiac was divided into twelve equal parts, which are the signs.

In Babylon, constellations gave their names to the sectors in which they were located during the first observations of the sky. Because of a phenomenon called "Precession of the Equinoxes," according to which the top-like movement the axis of the Earth makes at the moment the Sun crosses the celestial equator starts twenty minutes earlier each year,[1] today the signs do not correspond to the constellations they were once named after.

Each sector of the cycle, that is, each sign, has the characteristics of its position.

---

1 Being accumulated throughout 2,000 years, these 20 early minutes correspond to approximately one month. And that is why presently, at the start of spring, the Sun is going past the constellation of Pisces—not that of the ram, as it happened in ancient times. Source: http://revistagalileu.globo.com/Galileu/0,6993,ECT900784-1941-3,00.html

PART II
UP CLOSE AND PERSONAL:
GETTING TO KNOW YOUR SIGN

ARIES
MARCH 21ST - APRIL 20TH

Aries is the first sign, that which starts, triggers, drives everything that will make the wheel of existence spin and everything come to be. Everyone knows that this first push must be strong, determined, and objective. A strong effort is needed to push a broken car, open a soda bottle, and pedal a bicycle. After that, everything is easier.

Starting isn't easy. We think about the best way, the best angle, and the most appropriate words. If demands are really high, sometimes we don't get things started at all. That is why the beginning is always provisional, not very sophisticated. At a given point, we decide to get it started somehow. Refining and perfecting it comes later. That's the main feature of people of Aries.

The spirit of people of Aries has the characteristics required of pioneers. The first one is courage, because without courage we can't even get out of bed each morning. Then comes audacity, a little humbleness to accept that things cannot be perfect from the very beginning. Self-confidence is also needed to withstand criticism, which will ultimately come to strike people who take the initiative and act—you could always have done it better, of course.

For example, let's say a child is drowning. A person of Aries is a quick thinker. She calculates the risks, time and distance at unspeakable speed. She jumps in and saves the child. She reaches the shore and lets other people do CPR, since she may already have squeezed the child's neck a little too much. It's not her problem anymore. She did her job and is at peace with it.

People of Aries enjoy being the hero, doing something very hard or that nobody has ever done before. Just like children, drunks, and morons, people of Aries most often believe they are protected by the gods. Something deep in their hearts makes them believe that they have just arrived in this world, God's green Earth, and that is why they still have some innocence left to feel protected. That makes people of Aries not to like lying. It's just too much work to come up with a lie and keep people from finding out the truth. Lying makes them feel unsafe. People of Aries don't like spending time managing the consequences of their actions.

They say people of Aries are selfish, don't pay attention to what others say, or care about other people's problems. That they live their lives without looking around and don't appreciate the past—which is not true. Selfishness can be seen in people of any sign, who feel deprived, taken for granted, and needy. They stand there, their mouths open, waiting for someone else to nourish them of the substances they're lacking, and come to ease the pain. It is in the nature of people of Aries to have a strong impulse to move forward They can't dwell in the psychological maze of those around them, with their desires, guilt and repression, nor do they wish to participate in designing complex projects such as the new Pyramid of Cheops. They have no time for that.

Despite withstanding physical pain, our heroes of Aries are afraid of going to the dentist. They are persistent, and incurable romantics. Sometimes, they are afraid of the dark and hate horror stories. They don't run away from a fight, but get hurt by the violence arising from obscure feelings of inferiority. They love to love, because loving is a great adventure, and believe adventures can last a lifetime, until death brings them to a dignified end.

People of Aries are the #1, always first. Any person of Aries is naturally competitive and makes a point of coming in first place. They are not specifically ambitious, in that they wouldn't make all possible efforts to fight for power, money, prestige, or something else that would make someone stand out in society. What they want—what they really, really want—are the things that they personally consider to be important, from being the first one in the heart of their loved ones to having the fastest car (they love automobiles) or dating the most desired person around.

Everything related to Aries has a touch of precociousness, precipitation, unprecedented. They usually mature sexually earlier than the average age, which may be related to their tendency to be more on the shorter side, height wise. And there are also many cases of Arians who left home early, got married, or had kids when they were still very young. Actually, sex is something very important to this sign, because it is how they usually channel their energy. Men of Aries are usually very attractive and have very masculine traits in their behavior. However, when they're young, there is a risk they will be unable to offer pleasure to their partners, due to their eagerness to finish and the egocentric nature in which they face the sexual act. For women, the sign of Aries brings an advantage: they don't wait passively for others to give them pleasure—they seek it themselves. And they do it all without giving up their femininity.

People of Aries are bossy and like picking up a fight. They are bossy because they decide what they want before others and, consequently, their opinions always seem to prevail. And they like picking up a fight because they don't hold their tongue back when it comes to fighting for their space, which they do very vehemently sometimes.

However, it is not hard to make them see when they're wrong, if that's indeed the case. They accept it and there are no hard feelings. Actually, they don't really hold a grudge. Feeling hurt all the time takes too much energy and, despite being very active, people of Aries can also be very lazy... They are especially lazy in regards to things that are not part of their crucial interests.

These pioneering explorers and trailblazers aren't really patient, and lack diplomacy. Adventurers don't have time for such things in a real jungle, in their own private jungles, or when they're faced with the boredom of everyday life.

TAURUS
APRIL 21ST - MAY 20TH

Govinda is one of the names by which the Hindu god Krishna is known. It literally means "cowboy," "the owner of the cow"—the king of the world and all its riches. So, how come the symbol for Taurus is not a cow? I'm under the impression that, while cows have always represented wealth since ancient times, it is the bull who symbolizes the owner of all this wealth, which makes a world of difference. It is right to say that bulls and cows—their consort—share many characteristics, just as men and women do. They are the same species, cut from the same cloth. But it is the bull that owns it all.

People of Taurus are beautiful and harmonious, if not in their physical appearance, at least in their manners, the way they move, the look in their eyes and their tone of voice. Under normal temperature and pressure, the atmosphere that

surrounds them is sensual and pleasant, it gives us this feeling of placidity, firmness, and stability that makes us want to
hold them, especially when we feel insecure or needy. People
of Taurus usually don't speak much, so we speak for them.
They listen with an open, kind expression on their faces that
make us feel comfortable. Their preference for things that are
solid, long-lasting, and reliable makes them be there for others
when they're needed. People of Taurus are faithful to themselves and their things, including people—solid as a rock.

Taurus likes security, comfort, peace of mind. Taure-
ans would hate spending their life running left and right, getting things started, trying to rob Peter to pay Paul. That is why
change scares them—it inevitably brings instability. So they
patiently accumulate their wealth with material and non-ma-
terial things, with the perseverance and hard work required
to assure their peace of mind, which is not always possible,
especially when a person of Taurus is very stubborn.

And we know how hard-headed Taurus can be… But
everything is okay if their stubbornness doesn't exceed their
qualities and their need for material security does not become
greed and accumulation of so much property, money, people,
and pounds of fat that will become hard to handle. When this
greed is applied to people, that's when they find most of their
troubles. When they are in love, people of Taurus may think
that they own the person they love. After all, they offer ardent,
faithful love with a lot of care and gifts, a sincere desire that it
shall last forever. Consequently, what else would that person
need?

In both business and love, people of Taurus need to
have guarantees that they can fully trust others and will have
no unpleasant surprises in the future. However, only God
knows what the future shall hold, and there will ultimately
come the painful moment of suspicion that will awake in them

the ghost of jealousy—one of their most severe flaws.

It usually starts with their being in a bad mood and keeping a very long face. That's a horrible sign. This first stage is when they accumulate all their anger. If someone asks, they bark back, saying that everything is alright. The second stage brings the Taurus fury, which can be triggered by a futile reason, but comes like an earthquake. It's a blind rage and a tone of voice that seems to come from a medieval demon.

A friend of mine, a man of Taurus, once told me that he felt like a bull with bloodshot eyes, running around the ring, trying to exorcise his pain. Yes... the proverbial Taurus anger isn't something to be messed with. And just as much as they take long to explode, they also take long to calm down. When they see red, they have a hard time restoring that placid, docile look, and it only happens after some firm and very convincing evidence that they are indeed loved. It's more than words. I said they need *evidence*.

People of Taurus are strong both physically and spiritually, even though they are not especially connected to the abstract. They really trust their ability to work hard, persevere, and prosper. Taurus is a very fertile sign. Any seed they get their hands on has high chances of becoming a healthy, robust tree. Taurus likes giving life, making things grow.

There was once a Japanese researcher who came across a fossilized seed of lotus. Using much technique, patience, and perseverance, he made that seed germinate and bloom a beautiful pink flower. Had he been a Taurus, he would have transcended the issue of property and become happy forever, even after the flower wilted, he would know he had achieved something nobody could ever take away from him: his work, his art. And that is why we found so many men and women of Taurus connected to the arts. They make harmony stable, create transcending shapes, albeit fleeting, even if nobody can take it from them.

Actually, let there be justice: many people of Taurus have a fat bank account (as well as fat bodies) because they instinctively know what wealth means. It can be found in material things that, sooner or later, are irremediably perishable. It dwells on matter, but is not matter itself.

Here's a simple example: On a rainy Sunday, I was hanging out with a group of people and all we could do was watch an unimportant soccer match on TV. We were resigned to doing so, but this friend who is a woman of Taurus made a suggestion that was as simple as her own nature. She grabbed some cold beer, some olives, and cheese and said we could watch the game on mute, with some music on the background. She was skilled enough to magically change a boring afternoon into an exciting one, with good food, good drinks, and good conversation. She took nothing and turned it into something wealthy and plentiful. This is indeed the magic of Taurus, a sign that is strictly connected to nature and can make the most of what life on Earth has to offer.

But, here's a warning: people of Taurus tend to love their possessions so much—which they rightfully acquired with their hard work—that they may rest on them and become tyrants, when it comes to preventing the situation to change. They must learn from nature itself that everything is constantly evolving, including themselves and their own lives. Being passive and inactive is the second ghost that haunts this sign, and it's just as dangerous as anger and jealousy. Prominent figures in History have succumbed to this ghost.

Especially in what concerns people of Taurus, life goes on in infinite spirals. As these spirals aren't made of squares or straight lines, change is always required. Still, there is no need to worry and all can go on in a zen-like rhythm.

GEMINI
MAY 21ST - JUNE 20TH

Gemini are "in," and I don't mean they're fashionable or have good taste. Every person of Gemini knows if everyone is now listening to *funk*, rock, or 1960s ballads.

I bet when *kiwi*—that exotic fruit brown on the outside and green on the inside—first hit the grocery stores, most of those who rushed to buy it and try it were people of Gemini. And it's not about being a *gourmet*, because Gemini don't really care about food that much, but they'll put something new on their plate, even if it's only during a social event, just to show that they're "in." That's something very important to them: Being modern and never lagging behind when it comes to catching on to the newest sensation. Gemini love innovation, variety, and movement. They enjoy experimenting, testing, getting to know things better. In the very least, people of

Gemini need to know about the most recent events within their cultural environment.

If they live on a farmland, they know that a tractor is already obsolete and should be replaced. They heard from a couple of friends that a new model will come out, use state-of-the-art technology and be simpler to operate to make a farmer's job easier. It's impressive! Even if they don't do anything with that information, they need it at least to spread it around.

If you live in the city, ask people of Gemini what's "in" or "out" on whatever list of useless knowledge you may think of. In time, I don't have anything against useless knowledge, because it makes life more colorful and makes small talk more pleasant.

Actually, people of Gemini love conversing. They enjoy talking so much that they don't waste any time to stay current and learn about a variety of things, even if it's only superficially. Besides, they're very dynamic during a conversation. If someone changes the subject, they switch gears just fine and keep going. They only get upset when they have to sit through someone talking about things they know very deeply, or long speeches whose train of thought is hard to interrupt. And they're right when they feel this way, because this kind of people risk missing a good exchange and may induce sleep. However, since people of Gemini may have cards up their sleeve, they always do something funny to break the ice again. If there's no way out of a bad situation, they tiptoe their way out of it and go look for a better group to hang out with.

People of Gemini are intelligent. They're astute, curious, and practical. That is why every Gemini is an excellent interviewer. They can find the missing piece of the puzzle to give meaning to a story, concept, or current event.

When I'm watching TV—people of Gemini love acronyms, by the way—and I see someone asking a question among that herd of reporters hovering around an authority, all the while ignoring others shouting, pushing and shoving, I always think about Gemini. Most often, the interviewee is using metaphors and beating around the bush without getting to the point, speaking in jargons or sound bites, or simply resorting to rhetoric in a way that isn't easily understood by the general public: "We (they rarely speak in the first person) are already making proper contacts to urgently take measures, as soon as possible, in order to immediately address all concerns, yada, yada, yada..." Reporters then ask questions that all of us are dying to ask: "What contacts are those?"; "How urgent is urgently?"; "What concerns are those?". They try to get as many facts as possible from behind the smokescreen.

Someone who asks good questions not always knows how to answer them properly. A graceful woman of Gemini may be describing the wonderful time she spent in India, the peculiarities of the mystical Hindu society, the way people live there, the landscape, the religion, and make it sound like she lived there for over a decade, when she actually may have spent only two months in the country... People of Gemini are able to quickly associate things with utmost precision. They have information floating around in their mind, available for usage. In the middle of a very interesting conversation with so many funny details, someone may not be enjoying the story as much—be it a bitter realist or a megalomaniac who is upset at not having an opportunity to talk—and cuts off the speaker with a little bit of their same medicine: specific and objective questions. If the conversation is indeed great, a person of Gemini may lie and blow things out of proportion for the sake of entertainment. People of Gemini know better than anyone that life has its boring moments and it's always good to give it a little bit of charm and mystery.

When it comes to their love life, Gemini is known to

be inconsistent and superficial. It's just that there are so many interesting people in the world, you know? How does that one kiss? What about that one? Is he a giving lover? Oh, if only I could be in his life... Each person is his own universe of peculiarities and people of Gemini can't resist their curiosity. When someone is mysterious, it's even more tempting! People of Gemini gather around mysterious people as if they were devotees. They need to unveil all the attractive details behind that human being, as long as this mysterious person isn't really stupid... That's something that definitely breaks a Gemini's heart! *So all that mystery and silence were hiding a lack of smarts? A short mind? Obscure feelings that are hard to explain? Oh, the disappointment!*

Still, it's a small victory all the same. "We found it out!" one Gemini would say to another. "Someone who looked like gold outside is actually made of brass, just a fake mystery..."

That is why we must conclude that Gemini is a sociable sign that likes to communicate, has good sense of humor, easily adapts to any situation, is restless and a little disperse. Also, they usually have cute dimples or cleft chins.

CANCER
JUNE 21ST - JULY 22ND

People of Cancer are motherly. We can't talk about Cancer without talking about the past, our roots. Cancer is traditionally associated to dreams, the unreal, the fantastic, lunacy, madness, chimera, whims, sorcery and powerful occultism. It all makes sense and this is just so Cancer.

However, Cancer is a very ambiguous sign. I feel like using an ellipsis at the end of every sentence... It's a psychological sign and the subject of a conversation is part of the realm of the soul. We can say that Cancer gives us a soul, or purely exists because we have a soul.

Coming back down to Earth, as all other water-related signs, Cancer deals directly with emotions, and their main role is the pure and simple protection of the being—the human being, in this case. So paradoxical! And so it is. Emotions are meant to protect and maintain living beings.

In the most practical of ways, Cancer deals with our survival, which is a horrible word and such an ignoble subject. Our priority is precisely that, though: to survive. After that, we can be brilliant, important, geniuses. However, first we need to be afraid of fire and cold water, we must feed ourselves. Our emotional world cannot come crumbling down due to small controversies. We must withstand laws and loneliness... losses and frustration.

Right after birth, which is a violent event after such a peaceful life in the womb, we become victorious with our first inspiration, that marks our arrival in this world. We are a little blind, deaf, and completely mute—well, we can't really communicate with words, even though we can scream at the top of our lungs. From then on, we must keep ourselves alive. The round face, the big eyes, and the little movements to imitate humans are already very useful. They're very seductive and inspire the care of those who are responsible for newborns.

As it is completely helpless, the poor child sees its Mother for the first time as a God, or something similar. Upon feeling this strange pain in the stomach, a sweet and warm liquid comes into its mouth.

When solitude hurts so much, this warm body embraces us... Oh, it feels so good! But we didn't come here to talk about the adventures of a small baby. There are highly specialized books dedicated to this subject. Here, we're only using this event as a metaphor to illustrate the psychology behind Cancer.

People of Cancer are like a baby and its mother. Surviving is their motto. It's about survival at any cost. The crab is a very appropriate symbol for this sign, because it brings the archaic to mind: a soft center inside a hard shell. And, if need be, they walk backwards as well. They have "arms" that look tenacious and, once they embrace something, nobody can persuade them to let go.

People of Cancer are intuitive and instinctive. They know they can't survive all by themselves; they need to belong to a family, a tribe, a group that is united by blood so each member can protect one another. It's one for all and all for one. My tribe. For every person of Cancer, there's always *their* group and other groups. Naturally, my people deserve everything: forgiveness, understanding, and deep conversation. Everyone else gets the law of the jungle.

The keyword for Cancer is intimacy. Yes, intimacy assures a strong emotional bond between people, which are hard bonds to break, such as that of family, for example. Many parents reveal that they never stop worrying about their children, even when they're already adults and have their own children.

Cancer lives intensely in an emotional world. For people of Cancer, being accepted or rejected, mad, upset or touched is a significant part of their daily lives. It's part of "being with their head in the clouds," as most people say about them. Naturally, their emotional state has an impact on their actions. People of Cancer have mood swings all the time. The psychological universe flows and is flexible, one emotion can become another, and yet another, following external and internal stimuli. In other words, they may be happy, but then they notice that someone didn't give them the attention they expected. *Why was that? Is he mad at me? He doesn't like me anymore? Did I do something he didn't like?*

As they get worried, their face grows somber, but then they remember that their brother is returning from a trip and there'll be a party tonight to welcome him back. That's when they look up and say a nice "Good morning!" to a neighbor.

In a way, people of Cancer are always protecting themselves. They don't act openly, they don't talk much about what they want or intend to do. Nor do they tell right away that they didn't like something. They are subtle, albeit persistent and tenacious. When they set their minds to something, everyone better get out of their way!

People of Cancer don't really obey external laws, man-made laws. They follow the old rules of common sense and Nature. And it's all instinctively, of course. I don't mean that people of Cancer run red lights or lie on their tax returns more than the next guy. They actually do everything to a T so they don't risk being punished. They're not crazy at all; they're very practical indeed. However, if a neighbor complained about their child, rest assure that the neighbor is wrong, end of story.

A mother of Cancer doesn't want her little son to travel far away and can even get sick to prevent that trip. Seriously. Or she says something like, "That's okay, my son, you can go, but I may not be here anymore when you come back. My heart is so weak and all this heartbreak could just..."

People of Cancer actually invented emotional blackmail. They use and abuse this resource as if it were a craft and they masterfully move people. They know other people's weaknesses, which are usually common to everyone in the world, and jump at that. They could be great poets and expert storytellers.

Seduction is another strength of people of Cancer. An expressive look loaded with emotional charge is able to convince a large number of people to do exactly what they want. Still, this resource not always works in a fiercely competitive professional setting. That's when intimacy is no longer possible. Relationships are strictly formal and everyone uses a shield to face the battle. But that's okay, because people of Cancer are also experts when it comes to shields. Even when they're hurt, they put an armor on and keep on fighting.

Their memory is good. If you stepped on their toes or

humiliated them one day, you'll surely get what you deserve. It may take very, very long. But a Cancer revenge is the worst possible revenge there is. People of Cancer don't stick around, paying attention to when the other fails. They keep moving forward and believe in the cycles of Nature. One day, that damn person will need them. And that's when Cancer will turn their back on her as if it were the most natural thing in the world.

However, we can't really say that Cancer is vengeful. People of Cancer are worried about the basics, things that are essential and crucial to life. The social issues that usually move them are hunger, and abandoned children. It couldn't be any different, since they know better than anybody how important it is to be nourished well. And that includes affective nourishment. They know that hunger and lack of love can cut someone's life away or deform a human being that is still developing. No matter how wealthy they are, it always seems they have either experienced these needs in their gut, really seen them up close, or recalled that fact from their archaic memory.

That is why all other sophistication, needs, and desires seem trivial, purely a shell for the bare necessities. People of Cancer don't like when others complain, even though they have so much. When people of Cancer seem to be complaining, that's not quite it. They're only mumbling out of habit.

Leo

July 23th - August 22nd

Leo is the sign of love, that energy that comes from the heart and gives meaning to life. Loving is different than liking, which is a feeling that comes from affinity. Loving is different from feeling horny, which comes from opposites that attract each other. It is also different from passion, which is a projection from our soul into another person.

Loving is like the sun that shines naturally. And so do people of Leo. Love is there to be given. People of Leo go beyond and give their best because they have so much to give, even when they are shy.

If life hasn't been very welcoming and comforting, they can seem less communicative than another Leo who is more comfortable in the world. Nevertheless, when you look closely, you can see that pure generosity, which is something very moving: It's about giving without asking anything in return. One fine day, you get to work, sit at your desk, and see that someone left you a nice gift. You open it and remember having mentioned that you liked it. A person of Leo would want to be around to see your expression of joy.

How neat! Your day becomes a celebration, and it wasn't even your birthday! If you didn't quite like it, that's alright, and Leo can think of something better. They don't feel offended or have any hard, negative feelings, nor think about unpleasantries. People of Leo would rather eliminate any unpleasant possibilities and move on.

It is very hard for people of Leo to get hurt, because they always think they're the best thing since sliced bread. They like being recognized, admired, and loved. When they are centered, nothing really can affect them. If someone tells them that they're good for nothing, that all their thoughts are just garbage, they simply ignore that person for being an idiot, a poor bitter one.

However, when they are not so sure of themselves for not being able to be what they want, and mainly believing that they are underachieving their potential, they do get deeply hurt and could spiral down into serious depression. Their enthusiasm, which arises of their self-confidence and self-admiration, is the engine of their lives, the thermometer of their happiness. When they are enthusiastic, they can be very entrepreneurial. That's when they become productive, have several projects brewing, turn into a factory of ideas, and are willing to do anything. They make their dreams come true because their product—which can be either a child or the fruit of their creation—needs to be ready, visible, palpable and worthy of exhibition, so they can receive the praise they deserve and crave.

Since people of Leo believe to be unique, wholesome

beings and, consequently, capable of God-like creation, they extend the same concept to other people and expect them to be capable of doing something as well. That's when they may have some difficulty in understanding people's deficiencies, thus developing this tendency to think others are able to do more than they're actually doing. People of Leo then believe they are in their right to give advice and become some sort of a parental figure, which is an attitude that may not always be welcome.

Leo is also the sign of leisure. People of Leo want to have fun and think everything is so cool and dandy. That is why many of them love to be in the spotlight and are fond of everything that gets other people's attention, everything that is beautiful, shocking, and scandalous. Leo loves life and beauty, but it isn't only about aesthetic beauty and balanced forms; it's about the beauty of a gesture, a feeling, an action, and certain words. They love everything that moves people, everything that is touched by the divine, albeit fleeting, and reminds the world of the gods.

The "B" side of men and women of Leo comes down to trying to shine at any cost. Since childhood, they've always bragged: "I'm so cool. I'm the best. My father's car is better than yours. My mother is more beautiful. My house is the best in the entire world!" Then they learn how to defend themselves from irony, but can become a rug on which the people they admire could wipe their feet. On the other hand, they may become shy and dedicate themselves to planning a terrible revenge... For when they become the president or king of the world!

If they become unsuccessful adults—according to their own standards—people of Leo can become extravagant, like that guy who invites all his friends for a crazy night out and picks up the tab, even if he is bankrupt. If everybody is drinking whiskey, so will they—the higher the quality, the better. They'll choose the best place, the best of everything, even if it means it will be hell to pay back home. Actually, many men of Leo are considered by their friends to be great friends, but they're known to be tyrants in their homes, telling people what to do and becoming oppressors, beating their wives and kids for representing what they consider to be their misery, the reason for their failure.

Pride is another dangerous issue. Without pride, we become manipulated rag dolls, but excess pride causes very strong demands on others, including our children and ourselves. This pride can make people of Leo hide the fact that their father is poor, their mother is uneducated, their wife is ugly, or their husband is a layabout. People of Leo may hide their origins if they believe their hometown isn't hip enough. They can make it all increase their feelings of inferiority and may lie about their problems.

However, they feed higher feelings inside themselves, such as nobility, loyalty, hierarchy, and especially honor. It's all about the honor, because their hearts live in the time of the Crusades. That is why this sign is associated to games and sports. Hell is breaking lose out there, there's corruption to no end, but they're the ones calling checkmate on a game of chess. Inappellable. May the best player win!

They would sure like things to be this way... But what would happen to people with fewer abilities? People of Leo are for monarchy, not democracy, which belongs to Aquarius—their opposite sign. In the world of Leo, law is always respected, and it's the law of the strongest.

Everything is much more elegant in the world of Leo! On a tennis match, the winner always shakes the loser's hand. Nobody enjoys losing, but there must be elegance and respect for the game to take place—*noblesse oblige*, from the western saloons to a numbers racket. If you win, you win. If you lose, you lose. No sour face or complaining. The honor of players must be untouchable.

People of Leo find their balance in their heart, and things are very easy to classify. When they feel or were loved enough, they are a star, like the Sun. Pure gold. Those who were not or did not feel loved enough are like a disco ball, made of brass and with any tiny mirrors on the surface. Of course, as human beings, they sometimes show one side, sometimes the other... A wife of Leo whose husband is a useless piece of garbage could go around telling everybody that her husband is super powerful, and tells her what to do because he loves her so much.

People of Leo always take the nobles' side and do not admit any inferior intruders. Then it's a small step until they start sweet talking a superior or talking up a superficial contact they may have had with an important person, telling everybody that they're best friends now. Some claim they're even very close to the Pope! And that's how they may lose their train of thought about themselves, about their own idealism.

So, sons of the Sun, do shine! And give us, mere mortals, a chance to shine as well! Life only stops being a handful of trivial acts repeated to exhaustion if the romantic, excited, and even a little megalomaniac look of a person of Leo can elevate it above the level of mediocrity.

Without exaggeration, of course. And with a lot of love.

VIRGO
AUGUST 23RD - SEPTEMBER 22ND

People of Virgo know how to measure a pinch of salt. In other words, they know how to recognize, with utmost precision, that small and very important measurement that, there being too much or too little of it, would compromise the overall quality—as would the character of the very thing that is being contemplated.

French fries can only be called that by people of Virgo who enjoy eating them, if a set of requirements is met. I'm not sure exactly what these requirements are, but I suppose that simple potatoes that were cut lengthwise and thrown in a pan with bubbling oil, then drained and salted, do not represent ideal French fries for someone of Virgo. "That's not exactly it...," Virgo would say quietly, but with conviction. Of course, they didn't mean to offend the cook.

People of Virgo are like a very sensitive antenna that captures messages from all over the world with more details than other people. A woman of Virgo may walk into your house shyly and wait for you to indicate a place to sit. She'll rarely start up a conversation, but will talk animatedly later because she has paid attention to everything. While she was silently listening, she noticed you must have a dog, because of the smell of your carpet. Or she discreetly adjusted her position on the couch because she realized her friend sitting next to her was elbowing her every time he spoke, and she also picked up on different language flaws or vices everybody has, such as "you know?" or "isn't it?" or "Did you see X's clothes? So elegant, but the heel of her shoes was too worn out."

"Don't mind the mess, okay?" Too late, because she has already noticed everything. And might as well write a very detailed report when she gets home.

One of my friends is married to a woman of Virgo and, because he's so curious, he can't wait to get back home and listen to all the details of what has happened during her day. And don't worry, because she won't tell you a boring story. She has a sense of humor and is extremely critical and sarcastic. It's extremely funny to hear her talking about the dirty look she saw this housewife giving her husband, who was flattering a guest a little too much during the party. Or, what about that friend of theirs, who smokes like a chimney, leaving pyramids of ashes in the ashtray, along with all the dirt and smell, which she had to clean herself because nobody was doing anything about it?

People of Virgo can't stand lingering smells and dirt, and they don't care if they have to clean it up themselves. Actually, that's why people of Virgo are thought to be so helpful. Yes, they're helpful, but they're not driven by the generosity of their hearts or an inherent sense of cooperation. They seem helpful because they like keeping things in order. Besides, they believe nobody else can do these small trivial things better than themselves—or at least not the way they like it or think it's more efficient.

"What is this good for?" That's the first question, be it direct or indirect, that someone of Virgo faces when they are before something new. After all, if something is useless, impractical, or futile, if it doesn't take anyone anywhere, people of Virgo will not waste any time with it. If someone of Virgo is forced to participate in small talk, they will make sarcastic remarks the entire time, and sometimes other people don't even notice it.

Virgo is an intelligent and practical sign. It is very rational, but also very intuitive and instinctive. Because of their practicality, they apply their intelligence to everyday stuff: They know how to measure a pinch of salt—which no cookbook really indicates precisely—or the exact measurement of a container, because you must consider the environment in which things happen naturally for it to *really* work. For example, when it's hot, water evaporates more quickly.

Each gas burner offers unique heat intensity, and you also have to be familiar with the subject to know how much water you need to water certain plants in different seasons of the year... That's why people of Virgo are the ones responsible for "makeshift solutions." Can you believe it? Such a purist sign using "makeshift solutions?" I'm from Brazil, a country that was "born" under the sign of Virgo—our Independence Day is September 7th—and we are very familiar with this idea of "makeshift solutions," the Brazilian "*jeitinho!*"

Well, my fellow Brazilians, our philosophy that "there's always a way to do it" is a gift of wisdom and, as all gifts, it should be respected, and not manipulated to the advantage of a few individuals over a large group, that doesn't have the same opportunities.

Love and sex. Well, maybe we should say, sex and love. Women of Virgo are always dying to achieve sexual fulfillment. They're always worried they'll raise a red flag, that their heat can be noticed up close, just as they notice it in others. That's why they seem distant, mysterious, and glacial at times. Virgo is able to express with their faces and body the wrong message that they can live without sex—a virgin is always a virgin—even after getting married and having three children.

Her mask is sometimes so perfect that she seems to be intangible, an unattainable spinster. But that's just a first impression. The guy who didn't believe her Medusa looks found in her an ardent, delicate lover, although a little lonesome, as all virgin Greek goddesses are. "Sex is good…" we hear a woman of Virgo say. "But banality, rudeness, anxiety, and especially lack of tact are bad…"

Something similar happens to the men of Virgo. First, they are distressed for not being as bold as they believe they should be to win the heart of a woman. With time, they take advantage of being shy, subtle, always dodging everybody, and that's when they become very attractive.

There are so many details related to this sign that we could write several books about it. Maybe some other time…

LIBRA
SEPTEMBER 23RD - OCTOBER 22ND

Libra. The scale. The balance. It's all about keeping things balanced, right? One of the definitions for Libra in the dictionary is: "The ancient Roman pound, or unity of weight," also the latin word for the Roman version of the sterling pound (currency.) For "balance," I found the following: "A tool used to determine mass or weight of bodies." And also: "Prudence, moderation."

Libra or balance, this sign is, consequently, closely related to *measuring*—a standard used in order to purchase things. There's also a limit: You have to take measure, follow rules and norms that exist exactly for that purpose.

Do people of Libra spend their lives measuring, weighing, evaluating, balancing the scale? Or like a juggler? Well, it's a little bit of each. Most of the time, they aren't weighing an iron bar or a bag of beans, but something more subtle, such as human feelings, the duties and rights of each person in a relationship, a behavior that will allow for living well in a community, beauty, justice etc.

People of Libra are always looking for harmony, balance. That is why they polish a rough spot here, trim something else over there, and fill in the missing gaps. Their intention is to promote well-being, agreement, and middle ground. They are the kind of people who bring some coffee when the debate is getting heated, are selected to bring others together after a fight, or strike a deal when neither party is willing to give in.

People of Libra are born diplomats. They know that nobody gives anything away for free—there must be an exchange for an agreement to be reached—and that together we can accomplish more. And this idea applies to everything, from their love life to business.

Libra doesn't like extremes. Even though traditionally considered a romantic sign, and associated to marriage, a person of Libra hardly falls deeply in love with anyone, even though sometimes they say and think so. They would rather say they are "in love," meaning that they are "willing to build a beautiful relationship with someone they find so pleasant." Very extreme or violent feelings, be them of love or hate, do not let relationships flow nicely.

When they are in love, people of Libra are the lovers everyone always wanted: kind, collaborative, interested in what the other person does and likes. They usually give in more than you do, which can become dangerous. They give themselves and their things generously, but expect to receive the same in return, even though they don't complain every time they feel something is unfair. Actually, they let many things go to avoid a fight or putting a frown on someone's face.

They don't want to see others upset and wish that everything could seem in perfect harmony, if only in appearance alone. So, one day, as if nothing had happen—not to say "as coldly as they could"—they tell you in a very civilized manner that it's over, and you simply don't understand what went wrong. But, wasn't it all going so well? Yes, it seemed so, but that person of Libra hid all anger, hurt, disappointment, and headaches from you. What can you do? In such a scenario, people of Libra rarely change their minds.

People of Libra take very long to make a decision, because they spend so much time pondering all sides of the issue. They are even bothered when they must make a very serious decision that involves them personally, but once they make up their mind they rarely give it another thought.

Libra enjoys meeting a lot of people, spending time with them, because that's how they learn more about themselves. This is the party sign of the Zodiac, people that enjoy organizing meetings, gathering, and parties. And it's not only to have fun, but also to know who they can count on when they need help. People of Libra are always friends with someone who has invitations to special events, or they have a friend who's a lawyer, know somebody who knows somebody, and create a network of mutual help. Should we say that they're moved by interest? I wouldn't go that far; they know how to combine what is useful with what is pleasant.

They are often accused of being futile because they keep superficial relationships with certain people. That's not quite it: some people of Libra are futile, yes, but only those who feel like they haven't been properly appreciated, those who for one reason or another cling to appearances as if they were the most important gift they have. That's when their pride is limited to throwing parties—the most elegant and plentiful of the season—showing off clothes they bought in Paris, boasting about being friends with a member of Congress, something like that. There are people of Libra who have really lost their sense of balance.

People of Libra have a very refined sense of aesthetics and need beauty in their surroundings. They hate ugly things, bad words, bad manners, and negative feelings... Their house is usually pleasant to the eye, their clothes are adequate to their body type and social environment, and they instinctively know what matches what. They often choose a career related to arts.

However, there are a few people of Libra who dedicate themselves to the aesthetics of their interior world. As mentioned before, they often would rather deny their ugly parts and, in such case, not exercise their sense of diplomacy towards themselves. They are tyrants of beauty.

But, when they are dedicated to seeking interior balance by accepting their flaws, they become a role model for moderation, tolerance, peace, and prudence. So far, I have only met one person who seemed to be fully balanced in all areas of his life: a nice old man of Libra.

Scorpio
October 22nd - November 21st

There was a fire in a building. Everybody was screaming, tearing their hair out, thinking about their children, praying, repenting for their sins unable to breath. "Help, help!"

Amid chaos, someone remains cold-blooded, impassive, his head going a thousand miles per hour, his eyes with a hard, fearful expression. He has already evaluated the room temperature, the amount of toxic gases, the possible exits. In a matter of seconds, he already decided if he'll go downstairs or upstairs, trip, or throw himself out of the window. His mind is focused only on what's relevant to getting out of that situation, and he'll do everything possible and help everybody he can, the best he can. If he has to punch his hysterical friend in the face and drag him down the stairs, so be it. Naturally, he won't mind tearing his silk shirt, nor feel bad about leaving an old lady behind if she was only going to be slow and get in the way of everybody else.

Out on the streets, before anyone had a chance to thank him or make comments about the fact, he would have left already without leaving any traces. He will be alone for some time, away from the tragedy, and will hardly thank God for the fact that he is alive. His sign is Scorpio. It sounds like a crime and mystery movie, right?

Scorpio is really attuned to people who have death on their heels. People of Leo are aware that death follows them and could catch anyone of us at any time, suddenly, without any explanation. The way they act and live is the result of how aware people of Scorpio are about the end of things, about their own inexorable end: Death. They know death is around us, and it is implacable, irrational. There's no way of avoiding it.

One day, everything we have, everything we are will no longer be. Or, in the best-case scenario, it will become something so deeply mysterious there's no way of knowing what it will be or how it will be. Being aware of that, people of Scorpio usually opt to live and act like the man of Scorpio described above in the building on fire. If they live without wasting any time with frivolities—in this case, we're talking about a man and a woman of Scorpio who have set a goal to themselves, and are dedicated to it with their body, soul, and spirit—deep down they know they could just be one more person in the crowd; but they choose to become someone with special significance in the story.

While pursuing such goal, people of Scorpio are implacable and there's nothing that can stop them. Whatever the obstacle may be, they'll overcome it. Anything may be thrown at someone of Scorpio, and they'll deal with it while using the wisdom of the water that runs downhill: it doesn't retreat, it doesn't resist anything, and it only rolls down and around obstacles until it unfailingly reaches its target.

It even seems that I'm describing a Superman or Wonder Woman, but I do know some simple examples of this type of Scorpio in life and literature. Who could ever forget Scarlett O'Hara from "Gone With the Wind?" These people have accepted the fact that they are not eternal, while at the same time they have noticed that life is. And that's how Scorpio grows. They realize we fear death because we also fear mysteries and the unknown. There is something that radically escapes our control, our forecasts, and our standards.

If someone could control death, this person would undoubtedly be the most powerful person in the world. Therefore, whoever can control mysteries and the unknown, if only for a little bit, will already be able to enjoy a fraction of such power.

Let's say you're at a party and notice someone who's been keeping a hand in a fist for quite some time. After a little small talk, you ask about it and the person whispers that he unfortunately cannot tell you. Soon everybody will know that this person is carrying a mystery in his fist. "Is she crippled?" "Does she have a scar?" "Is she holding an important object?" People let their imagination run wild. Everybody would like to know and some would do anything to find out. Everybody goes back home from the party extremely excited about that story and there's great pleasure at dealing with the mystery—almost at a sexual level.

It is not by chance that Scorpio is often associated with sex: Without mystery, there's no pleasure, only that which is known and trivial. Maybe that's why the seduction of virginity may persist. Consequently, man and women of Scorpio bet high on their love life. Even though they may seem sadists, sometimes even mad, they just want to intensify pleasure.

A beautiful woman of Scorpio with magnetic eyes and naturally sinuous, discrete moves, oozes sensuality wherever she may go. She may even be absolutely horny, but will keep saying NO for the longest time. You don't understand it, because it seems that she wants you, and your desire just keeps growing. She cancels your date at the very last minute and it drives you crazy. That's how she keeps increasing the level of pleasure in the relationship. She's controlling herself and hopes you can do the same, so you two can escape the banality of mindless sex.

Sex is raw. And exposed. It's a moment of truth when the personal and social masks come down. Your expensive clothes get wrinkled, you get bed hair, and your most intimate moments are exhibited. And that is the favorite arena for people of Scorpio, because all secrets will then be revealed. No, unless that's their "thing," they don't have sex in public. What happens behind closed doors is a secret for those involved. That is why sex creates deep bonds between them.

A friend of mine, who is a psychoanalyst and has very strong Scorpio traits, said that he doesn't believe in people who say they have sex just for the sake of it, no strings attached. He assures that nobody is the same after a sexual encounter: There's always some sort of exchange of atoms and intimate fluids that change people, even if just a little bit. I don't know... I guess sexual experiences go beyond mere physical pleasure.

This sign is traditionally associated to money as well. Money is a changing value based on the exchange of goods: You buy and you sell. Actually, money is the last resort of seduction. In the absence of sexual appeal, we resort to money, which buys almost everything. But people of Scorpio aren't attached to money in order to achieve comfort, assure survival, or support their elderly mother. For them, money equals pleasure and, as a last resort, they pay for pleasure. And they enjoy the negotiation game, too. "How much is a house worth? What about a car?" That's not enough... People of Scorpio want to know how much a work of art or someone's dignity is worth. They love to evaluate honor, tradition, and abstract values. "Mr. Judas, would you exchange your loyalty for twenty coins? No? How about thirty? Oh, so your loyalty is worth thirty coins, as everybody was already aware of."

People of Scorpio can't accept the fact that they are mortals and get deeply upset by knowing that, in the end, they'll be six feet under and that's that. "No, no, no! That's so unfair!" It hurts deeply and there's no way of correcting it, because death will always be around the corner. People who are hurt can't accept that there are things beyond their control, including death.

As arrogant as a Fallen Angel, they want the world to change, they want rules to change. It should all be different. And there lies the root of their neurosis, which we must agree is where psyche gets stuck. But the world won't change according to their will, so they accept their revolt and transfer their feelings of being unfairly treated to another cause, that makes more sense to their personal history. If they represent a minority, that's where they'll channel their revolt. They can even think that, because they're poor, they're a minority—even when the majority is also poor.

This Scorpio gang is made up of members who are tormented, destructive, extremely cynical, *noir, gauche* throughout their lives. Still, that's a creative sign and, among all tormented souls, there are always examples of genius in all areas of art.

There is another type of Scorpio that is radically revolted. They don't accept playing the lamb of sacrifice, waiting for inevitable death. Instead, they kill themselves.

Scorpio is a sign of phases. It's about existential crises in and of itself, the opportunity we all have to transcend our material limits and give up acting like a child who tries to control the world. Transcending means finding freedom, accepting life as it is and trusting it blindly. But now we're getting into the realm of our next sign... Sagittarius!

SAGITTARIUS

de 22 de novembro a 21 de dezembro

"I'd like to believe that, deep down, there's always a sweeter side to a bitter taste," people of Sagittarius say. They always believe things will turn out right. And, no, they don't say that because they're silly. Intelligence is one of their biggest qualities, it's the good side of common sense, optimism, and trust in life... What a smart sign!

Well, not so much. They are as innocent as the other two fire signs: Aries and Leo. However, Sagittarius has transcended its own death—be it symbolic or real. There are plenty of stories of men and women of Sagittarius who almost died... But they're still happily living in this world.

Sagittarius is suspicious of the unknown. Intuitively, they know it is not over until it's over. Actually, they can assure you that it is so. They believe it so strongly that, oftentimes, they become travelers like Marco Polo, collecting messages from the far corners of the world, observing the manners and ways of other countries, other cultures. That is why their minds are so liberal, so benevolent, and not judgmental.

Morals and good customs change so much from one culture to the next! For an Eskimo man, it's polite to offer his own wife to a guest, along with food and everything else. Over here, if someone offers his wife, his guest will be suspicious—to say the least. Maybe there's something wrong with her...

Even when people of Scorpio aren't physically traveling, they may be taking a mental journey. Their minds associate logics to inspiration and common sense, thus creating a powerful intelligence that is the primary source of their vanity. Men and women of Sagittarius are extremely vain, convinced of their mental—and overall—superiority.

Their minds surely travel very far. Their excitement and enthusiasm are sufficient fuel to make them look at the future with an almost childish optimism, seeing thousands of possibilities, thousands of alternatives, thousands of opportunities. And that's why people of Sagittarius make a thousand plans and openly tell everybody about it.

Others often take advantage of their ideas more than people of Sagittarius themselves, and that is why they're known as people who talk a good game, but... Consequently, they are great when acting like teachers, even though that's not their trade. People of Sagittarius usually act like some sort of master and advisor to their friends. They're always willing to help. Well, if you have a problem that is burning through your brain cells, that's because you have no idea how someone from Japan would have addressed the issue. Really! And, whenever a plan doesn't quite work, Sagittarius always says, "It's okay, there's this other fantastic plan I thought of just now!"

People of Sagittarius like talking. Oh, and how they talk! Honestly, that's where some of their problems appear. They're excessively frank and may end up offending others. Their open-wide sincerity shocks some people, especially when they're being frank about themselves. Their beautiful, non-stop monologue—they don't let anybody else talk—may make listeners feel diminished and unappreciated. That is why this sign usually has lots of radical enemies and become the target of harsh criticism.

Thank God men and women of Sagittarius have a great sense of humor! They are the type of people that may be going through some hard times, but laugh at everything and at themselves all the time. Sagittarians are the first to laugh at themselves when they slip on a banana peel! Their sense of humor comes from their specific ability to project the future.

Think about someone going up to the mountains on a Friday night to escape the heat and responsibilities of the city. They are anxious to get there, see their friends, boyfriend/ girlfriend, and have some nice, hot soup under the stars... Then they get a flat tire and it starts to rain. "XYZ! That's impossible!" They get out of the car wearing their fake leather jacket, and start to make pathetic attempts at stopping someone on the road for help. Nothing. Nobody. They want to kick the tire and swear out loud. But that's when their magic sense of humor comes in. People of Sagittarius project their thoughts through space and time and can see everything from above, like the gods. *What a predicament you're in, my friend... Soaked through and through, asking for help, looking like a complete idiot. Later on, you'll get grease all over you, start to sweat, arrive there late... Well, if the spare tire isn't flat too, that is!* And that's when they start to laugh at their own sadness.

We, regular human beings, could think this is all funny, but well after the fact, when we're telling our friends all about it. We need time and distance to see how funny it is. People of Sagittarius start laughing then and there.

People of Sagittarius hate sadness, but sometimes get very depressed for longer periods of time, such as when they're hurt in their vanity or pride. That's when they can become rude, complete asses. They have fits of rage and, despite their size, audience, or stage, would rather just keep yelling, instead of getting physical. The most important thing is to yell louder than everybody else.

And, did I mention size? Not all people of Sagittarius are tall, but many of them like to act the part of big people with a bigger heart. In any way, when it comes to Sagittarius, everything comes in large proportions. Their expansive willingness doesn't tolerate anything that is stingy, small, obscure, and frugal. After all, you can't be a money-grubber when you're aiming for progress, development, and growth! People of Sagittarius have a tendency to be excessive in all areas. When seeking their own freedom, they sometimes go beyond that common sense they hold so dear!

Yeah... Men and women of Sagittarius have made a commitment to virtue and justice, which are measures of human behavior. We know radicalism can distort one or the other, but excess benevolence is also dangerous! Lack of sternness towards themselves and others can also make them unfair and resort to corruption. It becomes a matter of "Sure we can fit one more!" And, in the end, almost everything goes.

At a young age, people of Sagittarius are usually rebels. Well, there are so many obstacles to overcome and they lack so many resources... In order to accomplish anything, they always have to be subjected to such unfair rules and oppressive systems! And that's why they fight for their freedom like lions. Later on, after their belly is full and their bank account is healthy, they tend to become good representatives of the bourgeoisie and identify themselves with royalty—deep down, they were always part of royalty.

In order not to fall in the Sagittarius trap of giving in to excesses and cover absolutely *everything* there is to say about this sign, let's address one last thing I believe to be important. Men and women of Sagittarius always have one dream in life—a big, very ambitious dream. And they pursue it with all energy. This dream becomes a challenge to them; it's what keeps their lives going.

When we spend time with someone of Sagittarius, we learn that our accomplishments can never go beyond the size of our dream. In other words, a woman of Sagittarius who lives in the slums may believe that, one day, she'll be the Queen of Hip Hop, an international star. She may not get quite there, but she'll have a more fruitful life along the way than people who didn't dare to dream. And there's always a chance that you can actually make it. Those who dream small, despite living in a penthouse overlooking the ocean, won't go very far. Their lives will only be poor, like their dreams.

And there's nothing wrong with dreaming, right? For things to turn out well, all you need to do is have the wisdom to overcome frustration and humiliation with very good sense of humor—always. If you can't laugh at yourself, you can't pick up the pieces and move on.

CAPRICORN
DECEMBER 22ND - JANUARY 20TH

Capricorn always wears a nametag: "So what?" They don't like counting on that which is not 100% sure. They're no spectators, either. They want to be on the floor, with everybody. It's not a matter of having a special gift; it's about working hard for every little thing they own.

Capricorn is the sign that follows the road map to a T, and each step is completed with a lot of blood, sweat, and tears. Usually, from the time they were children, people of Capricorn had to face some hard times. Be it coincidence, synchronism, karma, or the result of their own actions, the thing is that life hasn't been easy on them. That's how they've learned there's no use in waiting for wishes to come true—you gotta make things happen. The weight of life's limitations rested on their shoulders from a very early age.

And it could have happened for several reasons: Maybe they were the oldest son, the youngest daughter, or the middle child. The thing is that they had to step up to the plate when they were very young and, consequently, they have faced some restrictions. Maybe their father was incompetent; maybe their mother was a tough general. Maybe they were from the poorer side of the family or something like it. It doesn't matter. From a tender age, people of Capricorn had to fight for everything they wanted. And that's why they are always suspicious of things that come cheap or are very easy. Something tells them that these things cannot be safe or last forever. "No, no, no... You're being very kind, but I'd rather be promoted through the regular channel, you know, after passing the exam. That's just how I roll!"

They look modest, don't they? Well, they aren't. *If I have to get to work, then I'll aim at the top of the mountain. Why not? It's a long and winding road I learned to travel. My journey has been slow-paced, but I'll get there someday.*

People of Capricorn have a strange thought process. Here's an example: They always expect the worse, so whatever comes of it will be something positive and they won't get frustrated. And why are they so afraid of getting frustrated? Because their heart hurts so much every time they're rejected and denied, every time their dreams fall to pieces. And that is why they're always aiming at perfection in everything they do. Perfect things cannot be rejected, ignored, and pushed aside.

In silence, people of Capricorn perfect their craft, which is a projection of themselves—and that's why it's so important. No matter how patient they must be, or all the sleepless nights and good get-togethers they'll end up missing. Their work will be beyond reproach and they'll make the world praise them and give them the glory they deserve. They'll face their pain and suffer with their loneliness in order to muster up the strength, self-confidence and love they need to grow as a person.

When they are observed from the outside, people of Capricorn seem tough. Their comments bring down the most romantic of dreams, and their advice is similar to those of a drill sergeant. But you better believe it's all for everybody's sake. They don't want you to waste any time or energy with silly things, just as they don't like wasting their own time and energy either. They seem to have no hard and be as impenetrable as rocks. Or maybe they are futile, fake, and have no emotional content. They give off the impression that making it to the top is the only thing that matters to them, or that they're very happy where they are and don't need anything or anyone.

I would not say a Capricorn's heart is tender. But I'd surely say it's rare, very sensitive, cherished like treasure. We need to defeat a two-headed beast in order to get the key that will open up their hearts to us.

People of Capricorn don't like wasting much time healing their wounded heart. Those who have a more romantic view of the world would ask, "But how could you have any control over it?"

"Well, you just can," people of Capricorn would reply. The only thing we need to do is learn how to withstand the pain caused by absence, to give up things that our heart has pointed out as dangerous—just like they do. There was this time when I heard the widow of a writer saying that, in her opinion, you can only talk about love after having lived together for thirty years! She may have been overreacting, but, for people of Capricorn, love is a feeling that is build, bit by bit, after years of communion, which must be enough time for lovers to learn how to welcome hidden treasures coming from the heart of their significant others, and give their own hidden treasures in return.

From childhood to adulthood, nobody truly loves somebody. People fall in love and project the image of an ideal lover on the other person, to the point that this image one day falls apart because the other person is never quite like we imagine them to be. And that's when we find the inevitable disappointment that, nowadays, leads to divorce and the search for another significant other, just to repeat the story all over again with a different character. Then we ultimately learn the difficult art of accepting others and loving them for what they are, just to be loved in return at the same rate, of course.

However, people of Capricorn aren't willing to go around so much. That is why sometimes they'd chose to remain celibate or tied to a purely formal marriage not to shake up their social or family structure, two things that are very important to them. It doesn't mean that men and women of Capricorn don't know how to love or give up very easily. In order to make the miracle of love happen, they just need to find someone with the same amount of patience and willingness to work on their feelings.

Capricorn is the finish line. Astrologically speaking, it's the sign that represents the highest point, just as Aries is the one that represents the beginning. Capricorn represents our impulse to achieve the highest possible ground within our abilities and resources. And we're not going to compare goals in terms of better or worse, more or less noble or important. A housewife who has achieved her goal giving her all has accomplished a valuable and dignified task that deserves the same level of attention of a scientist who will have his name immortalized in encyclopedias for having found the cure for AIDS.

Any life that fulfills its end possibilities, no matter how long or short, is beautiful and sacred. That is why the individual work of each person is painted with divine colors. A mother whispers to her children, as if they were at the church.

"Shhh! Daddy's working! Don't touch that paper!"

"You're allowed to miss special events if you're getting work done"—that's a Capricorn's motto.

Religions are sacred inasmuch as there was someone whose goal, whose work took place at the highest level of spirituality. But spirit is everywhere and work must be done equally. That is why our work is sacred, regardless of what religion means to us.

Therefore, people of Capricorn don't stop when faced with the first obstacle... Not even the tenth, sometimes hundredth, for that matter. It doesn't mean that they don't trust that which they don't see or aren't familiar with. They have faith in their own experience, their work, and time. Besides, they are real beasts when fighting the Devil, that is, if we believe that the Devil —or devils, "My name is Legion"—is in everything that makes things too easy, that tempts us with sloth or deviations, such as narcotics and intoxicating substances, which alleviates our tiredness and the pain we feel after struggling in life. People of Capricorn say no to these temptations.

As I mentioned before, Capricorn likes following a road map. Like Jesus Christ himself, who in my opinion was a true Capricorn and followed His sacred goal until the very end, without deviations. And He got there. His path was so perfect that He continues to be our role model to this day.

If we are astrologically tied to the wheel of birth, life, death, and rebirth—karma—, there is an exit up above, sideways. Once we reach Capricorn at the end of our own destination, we get a tangential path and we never go back. Well, at least the path isn't going to be the same we once knew. Maybe, like Jesus Christ, we'll get to come back in a new body, different, to live in another dimension.

AQUARIUS
JANUARY 21ST - FEBRUARY 19TH

People of Aquarius are weird... Always the odd ones out. Really, it's something hard to grasp. They are so nice, sweet, but they seem to be a king of smoke screen once we get closer. It seems there's nothing there that we can touch. And if we get to touch something, it's usually cold.

Like the other signs of Air—Libra and Gemini—Aquarius is the sign of communication and human relationships. But such weird relationships... The thing is that Aquarius has gone through obstacles while looking for protection, using others as a mirror to learn about himself, and used relationships as useful tools instead of simple relationships—it's a mere exchange of experiences and ideas, without any other intention.

It is the sign of friendship. *Oh, it's so great to be in a relationship without worrying about the other person's needs, whether they were offended, if they've offended you, if they want to see you bleed...* That is why people of Aquarius seem to be so cold. None of that actually flies with them. They are able to tell you off without offending you, because there was nothing personal in what they said. As adults, they were talking to another adult, in a completely civilized conversation. And, in case you've told them some harsh words, they're not going to feel offended for something so little. If things do get personal, they resort to madness, which paradoxically is how they defend themselves from emotional assault.

It is true that people of Aquarius have some tough skin. It always seems they are protected by a glass dome, which is invisible and indicates a line other people shall not cross, so they don't get too close. Inside their dome lies their domain.

You rarely hear people of Aquarius talking about intimacy. If someone asks, they say they're shy, and if you talk about your own personal life, they'll listen with empathy. Then they don't say anything, or tell you a joke, or maybe say you shouldn't worry about any of that. And they talk fast too, so they can change the subject.

They are the kind of people less likely to pick up a fight. People of Aquarius hate chaos, are always removed from the situation. They're immune, sometimes a little aseptic to protect themselves from the clingiest things in life. They can show you that they're not pleased with you by using only a few words, sometimes a single act, no strings attached. They don't mean to hurt you or offend you, touch you or move you; they just want to get the point across.

Because they need to be independent, it were people of Aquarius who created that whole story about "let's take a break." They say, "Wait, I need a break"—that is, when they say anything at all, because sometimes they don't even warn you; they just get up and leave. They are capable of going into a party, not talking to anyone, and then leave without being noticed. And nobody is offended by that.

Aquarius hates promiscuity and excess intimacy. They are capable of executing the most exotic juggling acts just to put an end to all that. They also hate when you try to explain things about themselves. That's when they do everything to show other sides that such a bold person never knew about. And it can be their ugliest side, too. They may start to belch, become very inconvenient, say or do a bunch of crazy stuff. The worst part of it is that they go back to normal as if nothing had happened. Actually, they know better than anybody that they have the power to be unexpected, unusual.

I have a friend of Aquarius who used to go on cross-country trips throughout Brazil on a bus. Her two young daughters were sitting on one side of the bus, and she was sitting on the other side, next to them. In the middle of the night, a child molester tried to touch the girls. As soon as my friend noticed it, she got up and turned on the lights. The man got to his feet too and, feeling that he had his back against the wall, started to call her every bad name in the book with a very hateful tone of voice. She then squeezed his forearm and firmly said, "Shut up!" The man did shut up and got off the bus the first chance he got. I'm sure he wasn't expecting that! He thought she was going to get hysterical, start arguing or crying. He never saw that perfect "Shut up" coming. Things that are unexpected have the power to stop people on their tracks and change the entire environment.

By now, you've probably noticed that "democracy" is a very Aquarius term. Everybody is grown-up and should have the same rights and responsibilities. People of Aquarius know that they're not an island, even though they are unique in their peculiarities. That is why it isn't hard to find them in the middle of groups related to social causes, carrying the flag of equality, liberty, and fraternity. They believe, as we should all believe, that we should not move away from the Earth that gives us so much, because we won't achieve real development by taking advantage of the weakest links. And that's something they're very serious about: Social and environmental unbalance is a threat to all human beings. And, even though people of Aquarius consider themselves to be superior, they do have an open mind and wider perspective, so they respect everybody. They love Mankind, because they're part of it.

The sign of Aquarius is against bosses, dominating and dominated, simply because it creates a wall between people that becomes very hard to cross, thus destroying the possibility of achieving fraternity, which is something we need so badly nowadays. I'll go as far as to say that, if powerful people don't realize that we all need to unite and, consequently, give up their poor, mediocre powers, we will all go down with this ship.

We are going into the Age of Aquarius. That's why the values represented by this sign will become clearer and be elevated, as we can already see. And there's a positive and a negative side to it.

On the positive side, the Aquarius propaganda tries to call our attention to the collective. The environment gets more space in the discussion and even the most close-minded people start to accept that we need to share the milk available in our own tribe, so other children in need can have access to it too.

On the negative side, everything is getting so cold, so Aquarius... We're dealing with human issues in a very sterile way, looking at them through computer screens and very cold statistics. We advocate for self-sufficiency as if we could foresee the great solitude that the future holds for us—the future of robots, loneliness, and state-of-the-art technology we see in the movies. And then there's violence, lots of it. There's ultra violence in close relationships, within the community itself.

Violence is part of the hidden world of Aquarius. The idea is that you must do everything you can for the common good, even if it means to destroy something. Lovely people of Aquarius could have horrifying ideas to improve the quality of life in the planet, and they'll shamelessly tell you about it, of course. If corruption is out of control, address it with ultra violence.

At a more personal level, people of Aquarius are usually very radical in their youth. Their transformational spirit wants to get back at a corrupt, rotten system with terrorism, bombs, and anonymous crimes. People are of no interest to them. Only facts are interesting.

Once they mature, people of Aquarius become very funny. They have a baffling sense of humor that channels their creativity in the most artistic way. With their peculiarities, people of Aquarius will always be cutting-edge artists and be more connected to the destiny of the society they're living in. They are socially responsible. And, nowadays, even people who are not of Aquarius have a hard time being removed from everything...

PISCES
FEBRUARY 20TH - MARCH 20TH

Pisces is on its way out. It's the last sign of the Zodiac and, like someone who went to a party, ate and drank, flirter and talked, and watched people doing all these things, they are tired, a little high, and dying to jump in bed and get some rest. But then, out of the blue, as mysterious as their dreams, the party starts all over again. The house is empty, everything is clean and tidied up, and the hosts are anxiously waiting for their guests. Completely astonished, without understanding anything, people of Pisces think, *I've seen this movie before!* They soon understand that there's no way out and they must relive everything one more time.

People of Pisces are born old. When we watch a child of Pisces, we can be really surprised by how often their comments are suddenly loaded with wisdom. Some other times, we notice that they have this unexpected condescending tone towards adults, as if they were the grownups themselves. They seem to see the precise line between serious subjects and trivialities. From an early age, they can't see someone who is upset without trying to console him, mostly with words, but also with affection and the most beautiful sign of understanding in their eyes. Actually, people of Pisces usually have magnificent eyes. They are so beautiful, captivating and resemble a very deep, peaceful lake.

They seem to know everything there is to know about human emotions. Everything we feel seems to resonate in their heart. And what a big heart it is! They can contain the anxiety of a teenager who will go on her first date, as well as the tormented soul of someone who has just committed the most hideous crime. These emotions that we usually reject, that we don't admit to ourselves, are completely acceptable to people of Pisces, and that's why they lack any prejudice. Who are they to judge anyone who acted a certain way that they may one day act if caught in the same situation?

A true person of Pisces will never join the bandwagon of those who segregate certain people because of their color or religion, the way they think or dress, or their sexual preferences. They know each human being is a complex and ever-changing universe in itself. Who are they to judge someone if they are aware that we barely know our emotions and how to deal with them? Besides, people of Pisces are very curious to know what people are like inside, and outside as well.

People of Pisces want to know how people live, react, feel, love, hate, and resign. Their curiosity is mostly geared towards those who aren't really part of their social environment. That is why sometimes we see a person of Pisces talking to a homeless, a transvestite, or a Hare Krishna. But their curiosity isn't merely analytical, because they aren't studying exotic human beings. They sincerely wish to experience a little piece of those lives they cannot live fully. Of course they wouldn't have time to be all the people in the world, and that's why many choose the theater and, even if they don't become actors, they act throughout their lives.

More than any other sign, people of Pisces need a *persona*, a personality that they can wear while living in this world, since they could just as well live off their gift like vagabonds. Even though some people of Pisces may select this option, which means that they don't give up their private world, other prefer to live the adventure that interior life represents. And that's how they create their persona and move on.

People of Pisces aren't frivolous. They take their role very seriously, which can change several times throughout their lives. But their true identity remains secret, sometimes even to themselves. And all people of Pisces have a fortress—a secret one—away from their private world of dreams and fantasies. That is where they play with and work on their emotions.

On the outside world, they do their best to seem like regular people. Even though everything to them seems to be relative—they find it difficult to make choices for themselves, since every single alternative seems to be so right an so wrong at the same time—they don't give much importance to mundane values. We see men and women of Pieces who are seriously making efforts to make money and be someone by acting in a very aggressive and competitive way, while running after very important goals without having any time left for anything. A woman of Pisces may defend her family with the same questionable criteria applied by a woman of Cancer, if she believes that is part of her role.

However, there are men and women of Pisces who

believe that this world is more hostile than they could withstand. They find a way to escape the mountain of imperfections and injustice and never give up trying to live in a perfect world that only exists in their imagination. They do not tolerate frustration or limits, and that is the category that includes drug addicts, parasites, petty criminals, and deluded people in general. Sometimes, in their delusions, they find someone, or a group of people, who convince them that being by their side is like being with God and having a fulfilling, thrilling, romantic life. That's when they start to follow these people or groups like an idol, to the point that they try to identify themselves with them and are at risk of no longer seeing their own identity clearly. In such cases, paradoxically, they may become religious fanatics, dangerous criminals, or any kind of useful innocent.

There's another group that doesn't accept imperfections in themselves, and these are the tormented people of Pisces, who fight against their own hostile feelings they believe to be the cause of their suffering or failure. They start to fight desperately to be good and end up creating psychological hell for themselves. They suffer too much, until they discover the miracle of forgiveness. That's when they're able to forgive themselves and others, relax, and learn that no error is a mortal sin and everything can be fixed. The only thing they need, though, is to be humble enough to realize that they're in the wrong.

In the Age of Pisces, that is reaching its end, Mankind lived through this dilemma of being caught between good and evil and having the responsibility to be good and avoid the terrible punishment of hell. Being good is achieving psychological well-being, being in peace with oneself. Being bad means psychological discomfort, caused by the guilt of not being perfect, not being God-like. Towards the end of this Age, the advent of Psychoanalysis has shed some light on these issues, and unveiled many of our feelings and emotions—the unknown desires we never even knew that were there, but acted upon us by interfering with our actions and shooting down the idea that all difficulties can be overcome by willingness.

It is only now that people of Pisces, as well as all of us, can start to go into this mysterious world of emotions and fantasy and sheepishly take our first steps inside it. And, thank God, it seems that the fantasy world knows no bounds through the oceanic eyes of people of Pisces. Mystery will always be there somewhere...

PART III
PLANETS

CHAPTER 1 - THE INFLUENCE OF PLANETS

As we have seen, signs represent different energies in action throughout a complete cycle. Planets represent the development of the Sun, the center of the solar system, as the colors that appear with the refraction of light. They are like children of the Sun, spinning around the celestial body that (probably) gave origin to them, acting as reference in their turn through space and providing life-sustaining energy.

Comparing human beings to the solar system—that is, comparing the human system to the solar system—we can feel in our bodies what functions correspond to the functions of the respective planet, since all systems are subject to the same cosmic laws.

Each sign is associated to a planet, known to rule a sign due to their affinity. Below is a list of signs and their ruling planets:

Aries ⇨ Mars

Taurus ⇨ Venus

Gemini ⇨ Mercury

Cancer ⇨ Moon

Leo ⇨ Sun

Virgo ⇨ Mercury

Libra ⇨ Venus

Scorpio ⇨ Pluto

Sagittarius ⇨ Jupiter

Capricorn ⇨ Saturn

Aquarius ⇨ Uranus

Pisces ⇨ Neptune

Each planet can be associated to a *sephirah* in the Kabbalah or to a Greek-Roman god. We could spend our entire lives studying a planet without ever going through all of its meanings. But, before we address each planet, I would like to make it clear that this book is not intended to discuss the deep, intimate nature of every archetype represented by each planet. Our intention is to establish a first contact with Astrology, an initiation, an introduction.

Planets are so important we couldn't leave them out of this book. We will talk about which roles each one of them influences us to play, what becomes easier or harder to deal with when one of these planets is more prominent in our astrological sign, or when a planet is in harmony with us at a given moment of our lives. Let's follow, then.

SUN - Its role is to promote self-consciousness and self-expression through creativity.

Positive aspects: happiness, nobility, beauty, luck, self-expression, vitality, enlightenment, will power, dignity, authority, righteousness, pride

Negative aspects: vanity, excessive pride, ostentation, oppressing those who are weaker, tyranny, presumption, susceptibility to criticism.

MOON - It regulates all of our psychic functions through memory and forgetting.

Positive aspects: emotional balance, active imagination, creation of myths, connection to the past and the mother, receptiveness, practicality, sympathy for the masses, protective instincts; relevance to childhood, children, women, and understanding the female universe.

Negative aspects: mood instability, complaining, mumbling, trivialization of everything, passivity, excessive caution, negativity, tendency to the whimsical, crying and emotional blackmailing, and lack of basic care with eating habits, clothing and personal hygiene.

MERCURY - Its role is to promote intellectual reflection and thoughts, building intelligence and skills related to associations, comparisons, communications, and speech.

Positive aspects: intelligence, adaptability, ease of communication (written or spoken,) collecting and distributing information, ability to learn, excite, incite, entertain, and play, as well as tendency to move the body.

Negative aspects: anxiety, restlessness, instability, indecision, lying, gossiping, slandering, astuteness, amorality, tendency to be an eternal child, lack of responsibility.

VENUS - Its role is to create relationships, seek harmony, attract other people, and promote well-being and comfort.

Positive aspects: ability to love, obtain pleasure and satisfaction, appreciation for the good things in life, being concerned with a good appearance and good manners.

Negative aspects: laziness, lack of responsibility, excessive reliance on others, parasitism, self-indulgence, selling-out, unwillingness to make an effort; using seduction to get that we want, and tendency to lust.

MARS - Its role is to establish and defend its own existential space, reacting to invasion, facing and fighting the enemy. Channeling aggressiveness and attributing notions of the weakest and the strongest. Impulses to act and get what we want. Sexual urges.

Positive aspects: energy, action, courage, competition, strong desires, passion, leadership, initiative, and intensity.

Negative aspects: intolerance, impatience, aggressiveness, violence, thinking that everything is settled by force, injustice, criminal or self-destructive tendencies.

JUPITER - Its role is to promote growth and expand personality and life. It creates the dream we want to turn into reality.

Positive aspects: notions of morals and justice, sense of humor, optimism, enthusiasm, sensibility, benevolence, generosity, tendency to preserve and defend the commonwealth; makes things easier and brings opportunities; promotes relaxation.

Negative aspects: excesses, exaggeration, corruption, self-indulgence, excess vanity, authoritarianism, and insisting in impossible dreams.

SATURN - Its role is to show that there are boundaries to life. It teaches us to withstand frustration and pain. It aims at perfecting human beings.

Positive aspects: interiorization, self-improvement, meditation, work, discipline, strength to face the tougher lessons in life, ambition, submission to fate, and accepting the cruel reality; perseverance and patience; wishing for silence and tranquility; concentration, circumspection; responsibility; sense of duty.

Negative aspects: Pessimism, loneliness, withdrawing from people, putting up an emotional wall, being cold and cruel, selfishness, unhappiness, not seeing what's right in front of our face, being hardheaded and suspicious of everything and everybody, considering others irresponsible. Depression, dark thoughts.

URANUS - Its role is to bring freedom through a compelling action or unexpected event, showing us that we're not just a number, that we are peculiar and stand out from everyone else.

Positive aspects: brings about a revolution, leaving the obsolete aside. Inspiration, quick ideas, creative genius, mental creativity, drastic changes, original thoughts, freedom from all standards; it liberates us from the past, gives us a taste of what's new, different, and original; desire to learn about the future; creating political ideologies and pushing for originality.

Negative aspects: Arrogance, revolt, anarchy, disrespect for rules, creating conscious criminals, eccentricity, anxiety, madness. It turns people destructive, perverted, scandalous, ultra violent, and extremists.

NEPTUNE - It's role is to awake in us the desire for a sense of accomplishment, peace, communion with God, and good will among Men. Spirituality.

Positive aspects: spirituality, faith, loving our neighbors, understanding, kindness, detachment from material values; psychic powers, extrasensory perceptions, taste for music and arts, making others be in touch with a world of dreams and fantasy, unleashing ancient emotions in us; it brings intuition, hyper sensibility, the ability to renounce and transcend limits and the human condition.

Negative aspects: confusion, dissolution, chaos, fear, despair, and insecurity; things are out of our control; tendency to use drugs or find another escape; neurosis, lack of emotional control, desolation, delusion, self-immolation, feeling like an outsider who is never welcome; feelings of guilt; self-punishment.

PLUTO - Its role is to bring to the light that which is hidden and repressed, and sending away everything that has served its purpose—or simply leave it to die. Cleaning and eliminating harmful waste.

Positive aspects: deep internal transformations, ability to manage power, understanding sexuality, cold reasoning, intensity, ability to enter any underworld, interest in the garbage and scum of the world; ability to go through an internal dark storm and make it to the other side, reborn.

Negative aspects: obsession, violence, death, end and definite, final experiences; sadism, a feeling that we lack everything; nothingness; absolute loneliness; suicide, terrorism; affliction, nausea, feeling the absurd.

Chapter 2 - Astrological Chart: The Moment of Destiny

An astrological chart works like a picture of the sky, as seen from Earth, at the moment and place of birth. It also includes an invisible part that, at that very moment, was below the horizon.

The smaller circle at the center of the chart represents Earth. The larger circle that surrounds it represents the Zodiac with its twelve signs.

The more or less horizontal line represents the horizon of birth and it usually goes through what we call ascendant sign, because it was ascending in the horizon at that moment in time, as if it were being "born" with the individual. Starting with the ascendant sign, twelve new divisions are determined. They are called "houses" and represent the main areas of our lives, as well as bring celestial events to a terrestrial context. The subject to which each house is related makes a strict analogy with the corresponding sign, in the order that follows the Zodiac division into twelve areas. The first house, for example, corresponds to the nature of the sign of Aries, which is the first sign, and so on and so forth.

Here are the signs, according to their order of appearance: Aries, Taurus, Gemini, Cancer, Leo, Virgo, Libra, Scorpio, Sagittarius, Capricorn, Aquarius, and Pisces.

Let's analyze a brief summary of the sectors of our lives that are represented by each one of the twelve houses:

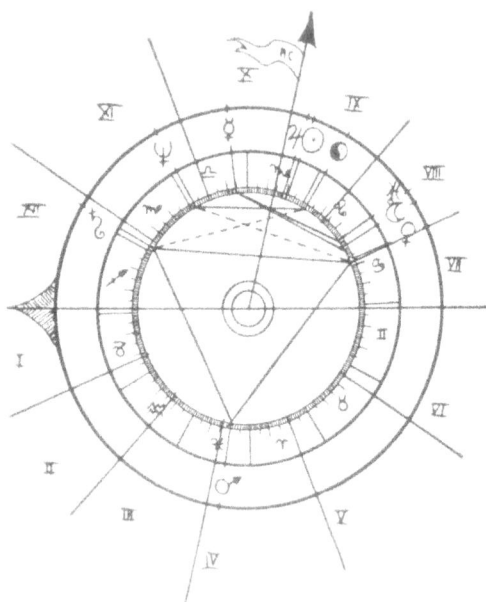

HOUSE 1: Personality. The way people will react to stimuli from the outside world. Physical Type. Determines the way people will present their first reaction to facts. Likes and preferences.

HOUSE 2: Property, possessions, estate, earthly pleasures, need for comfort and stability, money acquired through our own blood, sweat, and tears.

HOUSE 3: Communication, speech, writing, studying, small trips, family ties, brothers, sisters, parents, intellect and intelligence, information that is not acquired through studying, but by experiences on the streets, at school, and at work.

HOUSE 4: Dwelling, home, roots, past, mother, childhood, old age, family, intimate and personal life, emotion.

HOUSE 5: Entertainment, leisure, creativity, arts, sons and daughters, theater, romance, self-expression, exhibition, creation of the ego.

HOUSE 6: Work, health, employees or subordinates, everyday annoyances, learning through practice, ability to serve.

HOUSE 7: Relationships, marriage, business partnerships, relations with others in general. Establishing what our own family will be like. Enemies and rivals, advisors, doctors, and psychoanalysts.

HOUSE 8: Properties and possessions in common, inheritance, business, manipulating power, sex, death, and mysteries.

HOUSE 9: Higher education and far-away trips, morals, personal code of values, religion, foreign languages and all that is alien, dreams and aspirations.

HOUSE 10: Ambitions, social ascension, career or

profession, social status, sense of discipline and social image.

HOUSE 11: Personal development through debating and communicating one's own ideas, influence on society, friends, group of associations, clubs, and unions.

HOUSE 12: Mysticism, spiritual search, detachment from material things, sacrifices, illness, escapism, searching for peace.

Upon analyzing an astrological chart, we mainly deal with signs, planets, and mundane houses, as well as the arrangement and relations among them. Many people don't identify themselves so much with the description of their solar sign, since there are so many other factors that contribute to the peculiar way an individual is, and where fate will take them—which actually are strictly connected. We are not slaves to planetary arrangement; we actually build our destiny while using our personal tendencies the way it best suits us.

Let's consider a shy person of Virgo who was born with Uranus—a revolutionary and surprising planet—on her ascendant sign, which may be Sagittarius. If the ascendant sign receives influences and reacts to the charges of the world, thus shaping her personality, this Virgo person may seem more like an eccentric Sagittarius, who sometimes blushes when praised in public. However, she will still maintain that characteristic of easily learning the mechanisms that exist behind practical things, which is so typical of Virgo. She will be critical, observing, and essentially prefer things that are in order.

Analyzing an astrological chart is unveiling a mysterious world, when you can only take a peek at it here and there, through analogies, deductions, and synthesis that may develop themselves in infinite ways. You also need a lot of imagination and inspiration, of course. Does it sound difficult? Well, it is. But once you get the correct training, you can perfect your craft.

Chapter 3 - The Mystery of Human Relationships

I wonder if our signs match... After all we've studied so far, I believe we now know that our affinity does not depend only on whether our solar signs are in harmony.

Traditionally, signs were classified into three main groups:

— Male or female: Male signs tend to be active or direct, while female signs have a more receptive tendency.

— Cardinal, permanent, changeable: Cardinal signs drive things, while permanent signs resist change and become stable, and changeable signs are adaptable, mobile, and variable.

— Fire, Earth, Air, and Water: Fire signs are enthusiastic, Earth signs are practical, Air signs are intellectual and communicative, and Water signs are emotional.

Of course, the categories above are oversimplified, but they can be very useful during an interpretation.

Therefore, we used to say that signs that share the same element are more similar. In this way, Aries would be a good match to Leo and Sagittarius (fire.) Those with the same polarity (male or female) would stand a chance, and so would the ones with the same qualities (cardinal, permanent, and changeable.) And it all makes sense... Sort of. It seems reasonable to think that people of an emotional nature would have more affinity with others that also have an emotional nature. Therefore, since our solar sign expresses only one part of us—a very important part, by the way—we must compare the entire astrological chart of two people in order to check whether they have an affinity for each other, and what type of affinity it would be.

Let's take two charts as an example. She is a woman of Aquarius whose ascendant sign is Aquarius, and her Moon is in Capricorn. He is a man of Virgo whose ascendant sign is Sagittarius, and his Moon is in Leo. They have been married for over ten years, and get along just fine. Here are some of the reasons for that.

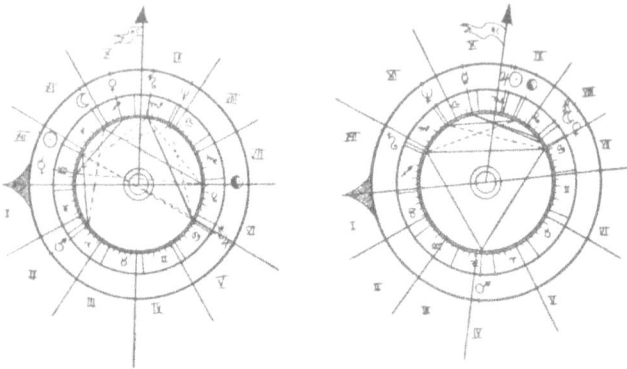

When transported to his chart, her Moon in Capricorn would be in House 1. So we can say that he understands her emotions, which are somewhat formal and constrained, because he also is a little constraint and formal in his own personality. Otherwise, he could feel rejected, because he expresses his emotions more broadly through his Moon in Leo and having Sagittarius as his ascendant sign, which are both expansive and demonstrative signs.

When transported to her chart, his Sun in Virgo would be in House 7, which represents the other, the partner, the associate, the spouse. Consequently, it is as if he were attracting her to a partnership in which she would keep her identity (Sun) firmly in Virgo. In other words, they would be united through work and the organization of their daily lives. From a romantic perspective, we could say that she sees him as her Sun, bringing life and joy to their relationship.

His Venus is opposite to her Sun, which causes an attraction that, at the same time, becomes a challenge. Her Venus is in the same sign as his ascendant (Sagittarius), which makes them feel comfortable in each other's presence. However, since she is in his House 12, which could only represent suffering and renunciation, or mysticism and peace, it indicates that their relationship represents a certain dosage of sacrifice, maybe even some hurt, or it is related to the mystical or religious. And so on and so forth.

In general, there are more indications of affinity than hostility, and we could say they're really a match. Still, that's not enough to assure that they would get married, or even go on a date. These are things that destiny keeps as a secret; and, under favorable circumstances, they were able to meet and decided to marry. If one lived here and the other on the other side of the world, maybe they would never have met.

Analyzing an astrological chart, one can understand many things, but nothing is set in stone. Someone can have her Sun in harmony with his Moon, which is a great signal of affinity. But, what if one's Saturn is in the other's ascendant sign? It is possible that they feel an intimate affinity, as if they already knew each other, but one of them will never be able to feel completely comfortable in the presence of the other—always feeling criticized or reprimanded in silence. Because Saturn (her repressive planet) is in resonance with the ascendant sign of the other person, she doesn't feel very comfortable with him.

I know a woman who has spent most of her life believing she was utterly incompetent to write anything, even a simple note. Her Mercury was in the mysterious and chaotic sign of Pisces, which nevertheless was in a highlighted position in her chart. One day, she struck a friendship with a young man who wrote a lot and started to write her letters. In retribution, she started to answer them. That was when she noticed she did write well indeed, and even felt pleasure in writing. She started to write poetry (Pisces if a very romantic sign,) and continues to write to this day.

On his chart, Jupiter was also in Pisces, and at the same degree as her Mercury. As we've studied, Jupiter is a planet whose action is expansive and creates growth and development. We can then say that he awoke her intellectual expression.

As we can figure out, it is very hard to judge whether a relationship between two people will be good or bad from an astrological point of view. However, we can understand how easy or difficult it would be to get along with someone. As usual, Astrology helps us clarify things, not determine them.

If you, the reader, liked what I wrote, it is possible that you will have an affinity for my way of thinking, the subjects that interest me, and the style of my work. You will surely have forgiven my flaws and imperfections and thought that everything was great. Otherwise, you would have several reasons to leave this book aside after reading the first few pages. Some (I hope only a few) would say, "I didn't like it because it's really bad!" Who am I to judge? What does "bad" actually mean? Some people like what's bad because of a shared affinity! And they may not like what many people say is good, because they aren't in harmony with them.

That is why I ask you to join me. You will be most welcome to come to my website, and my Facebook page, where you're also very welcome to leave your comments and impressions.

See you there! Peace to you all!